POURING

REFLECTIVE POEMS

Sharon A. Jones

POURING OF ALABASTER

Copyright © 2023 by Sharon A. Jones

All rights reserved. No part of this book may be reproduced or transmitted in any form or by any means without written permission of the author.

978-1-960756-03-9

DEDICATION

I salute the Divine Creator God, who has shared his power with us.

I salute my parents, Mary and Joe, in the small town of Coushatta, Louisiana

I salute mother Africa and the rich resources she has birthed on earth, especially the human family.

I dedicate this book to all my ancestors who inspired me to live a life that is rich with spiritual purpose, perseverance, and power.

FLOWING FROM MY HEART

CREATOR OF THE UNIVERSE 1

MY HEART 3

WAITING 5

DISTRACTIONS 7

EXPERIENCE 9

ACTION 10

DETOUR 11

HAND FULL OF CHANGE 13

HELP ME PLEASE 15

ROCK BOTTOM PLACE 16

SUDDENLY 18

THE ATMOSPHERE 19

WELL! 20

OBSERVING 21

THINKING 23

CLEANSING 24

ENCHANTED 25

DEPTHS OF MY SOUL 26

A PLACE OF THE ANCESTORS 28

EBONY GROOVE	29
I WAS BLESSED	31
VALUE YOUR SPIRIT	33
NEW BEGINNING	34
MISTAKE	36
QUIET	38
AWAKENED	39
SOLDIER	41
THIS TOO SHALL PASS	42
I MISS MY BOO	43
REVELATION	45
FLAMES	46
JOURNEY	48
BURIED DEEP	50
SAFE SECURE PLACE	52
DYNASTY	54
DIVINE ENCOUNTER	56
THE GIFT OF LIFE	58
FOUND MY SELF	59
THE INNER CHILD	61
REGULATE	63
MAGNIFICENT	64

WOMAN OF THE CROSS	65
WANDERING	67
SONGBIRD	69
USHERING THE SPIRIT	71
FEEL	72
SABOTAGE	73
GOOD THINGS	74
IDENTITY	75
NUMBNESS	78
The Place	80
QUEEN	81
SO MUCH MORE	82
RESTORATION OF LOVE	83
LIFT	85
Glory	86

CREATOR OF THE UNIVERSE

Deep within the
well of my soul,
a mysterious
creative sacred workshop resides
to repair my brokenness,
to fill the holes.
It is way beyond
physical eyes.
It is in a magical realm.
You cannot see.
Led by great spirits,
working endlessly,
far away from earth, are
the master blueprints,
the true identity,
the opposite of what
my feelings keep,
telling me
what my words say
when I cannot see my way.

Left alone and abandoned,
I do not know where to turn.
Joyless without any fun,
I cannot imagine
a brighter day.
On days like this,
I feel like my spirit,
is submerged below water.
Like a submarine,
I have lost my divine guidance.
I am feeling
lost, from afar it seems
I need a tugboat
to tow me back
to my true destiny.
So that I can see
who made me
or loved me first?
Is it the Creator of the
Universe?
It is.

MY HEART

My heart is filled
with uncertainty,
trying to understand
what is the best
path for me.
I have been walking
for such a while,
trying to learn
my rhythm and style.
Not all the time
I could smile.
I see others,
capturing
their BIG dream,
but it seems like
I am so far off course.
I cannot find my most.
The heart has
a silent message
that keeps on speaking.
But it is hard to listen.
Sometimes the doubt
begins to glisten,
chaos sets in,
blots the message out.
And so begins a cycle
of not knowing

how to win.
This is the uncertain part,
that is always causing
me to check
my heart.

WAITING

As I sit and waited,
I started
to reminisce
about all the things
I hated
about me.
The positives
I could not see.
My mind, body,
and spirit
just did not agree.
I was out
of alignment.
Too much time
on negativity,
blocking and clouding
my view,
leaving me to hope less,
where I did not know
just what to do.
There was a veil
between lies and truth.
So, I waited,
frustrated,
consumed by thought,
that were back dated,

had already
happened,
were beyond
my control.
I could see no
end in view.
Yet and still
I waited.

DISTRACTIONS

I am off course.
I cannot see or find my way.
Confusion has set in.
I do not know what day
it was.
I am in life.
I am loss.
My thoughts and feelings
are the boss
of my life.
I am overpowered.
Pressed down.
My thoughts are overflowing.
I need help.
Forgive me, for not knowing
which way to turn.
I cannot recognize
where I am.
But I know,
I need to take
positive action.
Yet there are
so many distractions,
and the only
remedy is to be free
of the interruptions.

Detour and distractions
that hold and bind me!
Time to focus,
free of charge
and step into action.
Leaving behind all
distractions.

EXPERIENCE

I have stepped
back in time,
but time
is an illusion.
A ghost of
the mind,
of the here
and now.
Leading to
major confusion,
reflections on life,
like the playing
and making
of a movie.
The different
channels,
the flipping
back and forth,
consuming time,
moments in life,
building up courage
through dollars
and sense.
Such a rare valuable
experience.

ACTION

I am stuck
in a deep well.
I cannot look up.
I have no traction.
I have taken
on too much.
I am overwhelmed,
in a rut.
I wish the flames
would arrive
to spark my
Midas touch.
That instant
manifestation
of being.
Filled with so much.
Fire to ignite
my life,
and move into
action.

DETOUR

I am aware of
the Divine.
That pure perfect
moment in time.
It is not
a curving line,
but straight truth
that helps our light
to shine.
Illuminates our view,
so we do not curve
off the road.
The Path
gets lost, I lose sight.
Wander through
the night,
unable to find
our way,
or figure things out.
Each way feels
like the right way.
I am losing energy.
I do not know
my location in life.
I feel the strife.
I am spinning

off course.
I need more
understanding.
My GPS is broken.
I am not sure.
I have experienced
a detour.

HAND FULL OF CHANGE

It started with
a simple invite.
When hope
was locked,
in and out of sight,
faith and courage
were stirred up.
So, I got up and
asked for help.
So, I could take
that first step.
My father
did his best.
He gave me.
all he had.
A hand full
of change,
I traveled from
the South
to the West
alone, and
not knowing
what to expect.
Just trying to
pass the test,
that life had

presented to me.
I gave it a chance.
Flowed with
the unknown.
Looked for a
better way,
which paved
a better day.
Remembered
the exchange,
the hand
full of change.

HELP ME PLEASE

I kneeled to pray.
I had an absence of faith.
I hoped for miracles,
signs, and wonders.
I held on tight,
trying not to go under.
I felt down and out.
I remembered
the power of words
So, I began to shout.
I remembered
that you could
declare and decree a thing,
and restore your dream.
So I cried out, and
the weight lifted.
I felt at ease.
The words I said were,
Help me please.
Help me please.
Oh God, please
help me,
please.

ROCK BOTTOM PLACE

As I leaned down
to pick up the beautiful
iridescent blue rock,
I noticed
I was at the bottom.
Too weighed down
to look up and around.
Bad thoughts, feelings,
and disappointments
got me down.
Too bound to look ahead.
My right is filled with shame.
My left is a path of pain.
Holding back the tears,
no more to shed,
head hung down,
view is restricted blocked.
Filled with dread,
I could not clearly see.
All I could see
was destruction and avarice.
All I could hear was run around,
find your way,
before you are found.
My heart was filled with hurt.
Scars on the inside,

feeling like dirt,
bursting with fear,
afraid of being destroyed.
I began moving
away from the past,
but the obstacle
was too high.
I struggled to overcome.
Started to give up
and not try.
Looking for the best turn
by pouring out
my fear and disgrace.
I was able to leave my
rock bottom place.

SUDDENLY

My world has changed.
Things are happening to me
that I cannot explain.
It came upon me
all of a sudden.
Looks like the universe
just pushed the magic button,
but I am stuck.
My spirit cannot receive.
My thoughts still deceive.
I know that everything
is within arm's reach.
It is so hard
to believe
that things have changed,
everything rearranged.
I walk different.
I think different.
I am brand new.
I can finally be
Me.

THE ATMOSPHERE

It is time to change
the atmosphere.
To shake up
the status quo.
To find that
healing flow.
To usher in
positive energy.
To release a
beautiful fragrance.
To stir up the
spirit of Synergy.
So, I can have
a fair chance
to feel the
energy of hope,
by breaking
the boxes
that restrict
and contain,
like a yoke,
my mind, body,
and spirit
that keep creating
the atmosphere.

ALL IS WELL!

Something happened
to me
that shook the
inner part of me.
I struggled just to be.
I went in the four
corners of my mind.
Trying to align my body.
Trying to be free.
I became frustrated.
I got overwhelmed,
the fear became
overrated,
where I could
not take it.
It was like receiving
a bad letter
in the mail.
It was like a story
with no ending
that I could tell.
I revived my intention,
improved my condition,
gave my life
the benediction,
ALL IS WELL!

OBSERVING

I am looking,
not seeing clearly.
I am confused.
In a place of
being used
by my own set rules
of the game.
Sunken by connecting
with the shame.
I am looking.
My eyes are closed.
I do not have the strength
to play the game.
So much time is spent
on power,
struggles, and nonsense.
I am stepping out
of the frame
to move
beyond
playing games.
Embracing love
and gratitude.
Changing up the rules.
Spirit is my anchor,
my guide,

telling me to
focus on my breath.
There is nothing left,
but the gifts
from above
that gives me life.
That is what
I have observed!

THINKING

I am thinking
about
all that junk
and harmful stuff.
I am looking at all
that is not good.
I cannot get to
a place of should.
I carry so much.
Let it define
who I am
and who I should be.
While I walk on
through my destiny,
I am thinking.
How to stay afloat,
be strong,
and not sink
into the rhythm
and flow
that says no.
You should do this.
What if
it's not so true,
only a part
and reflection of you

CLEANSING

I tried to center myself,
but I was so filled
with experiences
that told me
I was not enough,
that left me abandoned
with no help,
I felt alone.
Way down at the cellular level,
at my core.
It would need a shovel
to dig up the old pieces.
So, I could continue to grow.
I sent intentions,
asking to rain down
the good stuff
Like rain falling
in a season of drought.
So refreshing, uplifting,
and invigorating.
I felt like I had left.
Rejected the old spirit.
It was no longer listening.
Filled with so much
positive renewal.
I received my cleansing.

ENCHANTED

Sometimes I feel
so mesmerized.
by the goodness in life.
I am charmed
by the wisdom
of those I meet.
It is so timely,
like a tasty, delicious treat.
I am captivated
by the power of words
and knowledge
from inside and above.
The language of love
that brings gifts
and not baggage.
A great investment
we all should have.
It adds value,
helps you find your way,
when walking
in the wilderness.
Access is granted,
even when you
are walking
through the
enchanted.

DEPTHS OF MY SOUL

There is an invisible place.
There is an empty space.
That needs to be filled with grace.
It is about spiritual things.
It is about being whole.
It is about repairing
the holes in our soul.
Like feeling something
is missing.
Something is absent.
Something is working
out of you,
but it is out of view.
It is like a reservoir
that has little water.
You are in need,
but you do not know
what to do.
It is a deep
conversation with self
of self.
It is a conversation
from within.
It can only be filled
up by replacing the old.
It is a silent conversation

with the power of spirit,
and the soul.
We can feel it operating,
and we do not know
how to connect.
Many say you must be bold.
In line with the holy scriptures
to connect your soul.
It runs deep, it runs wide,
like an operating system
on the computer,
you cannot see.
It can be uncertain.
When you reach out
to God for help,
not knowing
what will it be?
Feeling like there
is nothing left,
feeling life has
turned cold, empty.
That is when you reach
deeper depths of your soul

A PLACE OF THE ANCESTORS

I wonder all day long,
Where my ancestors have gone.
Some say they are
in another dimension,
but I cannot see them,
or get their attention.
There are so many memories,
some were gone too soon.
The flower was picked,
before they could bloom,
before they could walk in the rain.
Things happen,
things change,
there is a longing
in the soul
to reconnect,
to find that perfectness,
to reconnect,
to restore the relationship.
I look for signs and tips.
Say hello,
or drop a leaf on my head.
I just want to know if you're listening.

EBONY GROOVE

Let me introduce you
to Ebony land.
Not just to hit it
and quit it
after a minute,
but to stay awhile
to get to know
the great richness
of Ebony style.
To experience the richness
of warmth in winter,
coolness in summer
growth in spring.
To be taken away
like a beautiful dream,
to have an encounter
of Ebony richness.
How we speak, move
to the beat
of the Ebony groove.
It is like no other,
for we have deep deep roots.
It is like no other, for we get
it from our mother.
All the curves and thickness,
the richness of color,

so beautiful to the eye,
so soft to the touch,
so stimulating to the
mind, body, and soul.
It is so wonderful,
pleasing and smooth,
like no other,
when taken higher
True love fulfilled
with passion and desire,
when you encounter
The Ebony Groove

I WAS BLESSED

To have a grandmother
called Mama honey.
She was quiet.
Loved her family.
Remembered her friends.
She prayed a lot.
Taught me how to
live within.
She used the gift of prayer.
She knew
the Author
of air and wind.
She respected
the giver of breath and life.
She was spiritually connected.
She was always nice.
She taught me,
there are some places,
we cannot go naturally.
It is a journey
through the soul.
A land of mystery.
That was way
before our history
on earth, our natural birth.
It is beyond the sky.

You cannot GPS it.
So do not bother to try.
You must turn within
to access it
You must clear
out the sin.
The things that
are not right.
Only you know
what will restore.
Your life flows
and connect you to
the marvelous light.

VALUE YOUR SPIRIT

There is nothing better
than a healthy spirit.
That way, you can hear,
see your instructions for life,
feel the connection
in your soul.
Fill the empty holes
so you do not walk abound.
Trapped, not able to align
with your faith,
feel safe and fill your space
with love and goodness.
Be aware of the right
walk-in life.
Be certain so you
do not have to think twice.
Stay aligned with the prize,
walk through life being nice,
changing the atmosphere,
sharing a message
for all to hear
how you value your spirit.

NEW BEGINNING

Have you ever
begun to think
that you have done
everything wrong?
That your energy is low.
All your passion is gone.
You go into the four corners
of your mind,
searching to find
that invisible power
that is fueled
by the divine
but your body and your soul
keeps telling your spirit,
there is nothing but holes.
You are not winning.
It feels like life
is spinning in your mind.
You feel chaos.
Everything is just shaking.
So, your energy begins
to increase
like an earthquake.
Situations are bouncing,
moving you back and forth.
You find yourself

in that low place,
trying to figure out
how to access grace
to lift you from the lowly place,
to rise and cope,
to access more hope,
where things were perfect.
Like in the beginning,
new beginning.

MISTAKE

My early learning,
a strong and powerful foundation,
my fearless ancestors
told me that I would rise up
and impact the nation.
Then life happened.
I needed more information.
You see, it is a big old world
out there, and sometimes
you meet people
that are just faking.
Just like a faulty
navigation system,
they may guide you
the wrong way.
Instead of being
in a motion picture,
you end up in a
dysfunctional play.
Before you know it,
you realize that,
you have traveled far
off the grid
and the many choices,
you have made.
You are filled with shame,

hearing the wrong voices
of chance encounters.
Brings a different message,
that second chances do happen.
You can live strong again.
The charges have been dropped.
There is nothing on your plate.
Canceled, no more
mistakes.

QUIET

It is too quiet,
so I need more.
My life has been
declared a great bore.
I stopped living.
Holding firmly,
hiding my gifts,
not even giving.
Everything is stuck
in a spiral.
Down to the ground.
Now the reflection is on.
What could have been done?
To spread the benefits
I need to get
to myself, look inner,
away from the chaos,
and the mess.
I need to get
to my quietness

AWAKENED

I suddenly woke up
from tossing and turning
in my sleep.
I noticed that
my thoughts
were getting deep.
You know life can
have you thinking
about many things.
Sometimes it leads to us.
Putting up barriers
to precious dreams.
You know life can
bring us a lot of
different situations
that can disrupt
and keep you up at night
so much that you
ask yourself,
what is up?
Your heart yearns
and burns,
longs for what might be
the possibility of victory.
But something
about that energy

keeps the world spinning.
You try to fall
back asleep,
but you just
cannot sleep.
You begin to
pray and shake.
You receive
great insight
that keeps you
awake.

SOLDIER

You are a soldier.
You are already together.
I do not need to mold you.
There is nothing better.
You come up from
the bottom, the streets.
You are so hard, yet so sweet.
Yes, you are marching
to that soldier beat.
You are so much of a bargain.
You can keep it real,
and you are not cheap.
Oh, such manpower.
Can you hear that beat?
Clean cut, shaven,
crisp and neat.
Willing to take on a challenge.
Not afraid of defeat,
hearing that marching sound.
Ready to throw down.
Soldier, Soldier,
I hear you, feel you.
I know
you are doing your thang.
Ready on the go!

THIS TOO SHALL PASS

My mind worries
all the time.
It is like a clock
with a fast chime.
I try to refocus,
think of something new,
the energy gets so intense,
I do not know what to do.
My mind is filled with
what ifs.
Moving so fast,
I met a spiritual teacher
who told me,
things are never as
bad as they seem.
The sun will rise
new mercies every day.
Troubles do not last.
This too shall pass.

I MISS MY BOO

Don't you think I know
what you are going through?
Sometimes it is so hard.
Having free time to look at you.
When all your thoughts,
feelings, heart and soul,
tell you, Boo is better
than gold.
Don't you know?
It is hard being alone
when the love
of your life is gone.
When time suddenly
become yours to
do whatever you want.
And in the past
all you heard was don't.
Holding someone
else higher
than your wants and desire.
You are taken to that
place of emptiness, a void.
The pain is so deep,
you reach out to God.
Then you find out, it is not hard.
It is meant for you

to play the game smart,
then you focus
and understand.
that your Boo
was not even a man.
Only a little boy
with an underdeveloped
heart and plan.
Then you raise
your hand to God
and apologize for being so blind.
You renew the four corners
of your mind.
Your thoughts become
so simple, intelligent,
and plain.
Because your whole heart,
has changed and grew.
You no longer
miss your Boo.
But you decide
to redefine your life
and do you.

REVELATION

I woke up this morning
with low energy to get up.
My first thought was, what's up?
I see people who are joyous
in life, despite the strife.
I see people enjoying life,
despite not having.
It's a better way.
So I stopped.
Focused, paused,
and hit reset.
I understand,
what you think
about you.
So, I reset the vibration
to a more positive station
to a day that
is filled with elevation.
Seeing through,
the eyes of gratitude
to a day that is focused
on divine revelation.

FLAMES

As I stretch
out my arms,
I flipped my hands
and looked
at my palms
to see what
I could see.
Looking into my eternity,
that life sometimes can be
an illusion,
playing tricks on me,
where I am left
in confusion,
with so many thoughts.
Moments in life,
trying to keep
myself together.
Walking through
the shame,
trying to address
the pain,
knowing that my mind
is not the same.
I remember to return
within my core self,
to get rid of the blame,

to begin to praise the good.
My energy started to raise,
so there I stood.
Stronger, but feeling the same.
My focus got better,
increasing my aim.
So I stretched out my arms,
flip them over to
see my palms, to my surprise.
Things were strange.
I was standing even stronger.
Feeling like I had risen.
My vision was clear.
My hands look new.
They were not the same.
I noticed my hands.
They were flames!

JOURNEY

When I journey back
to that place, referred to as past
I have reflections
of many things I need to erase.
So, they won't last,
but my mind
is slow to release
an atmosphere of peace.
I seek and cannot find.
My mind is like an ocean,
moving back and forth
with chaos and commotion.
Oh, if someone
could help me enjoy,
the here and now,
lead me to
that place of WOW,
illuminate wisdom and truth,
create a safe space,
strengthen my faith,
give me the proof,
where I can lay down
in the loving arms
of God's Grace.
As you know
it is difficult to run this race.

Find your true essence.
Hold up the beautiful
sparkly vibrant jewels
in a perfect crown
that reflect his presence.
Rain it all down
in the four corners
of the mind.
From eternity to time
where the eyes can see
the perfect divine
destiny on the JOURNEY.

BURIED DEEP

Buried deep
inside of me
is a picture.
I am filled with dreams
of what could be?
Many seeds have
been planted.
I am ready
for them to grow.
Ready for the
big harvest,
to access all my gifts.
Time for them to show,
but they are hidden away.
I am in a period of waiting.
Trying to focus and stay.
I add the secret ingredient
of trust to
activate my faith.
To guide me
to all possibilities.
It is the catalyst.
for all that will be.
The plan that
will determine
my legacy.

It operates in the invisible,
out of the sight
of human eyes.
It operates
in another realm,
way beyond the skies.
My divine design,
my identity,
where our God Spirit
is at the helm.
The great giver of life,
the most precious gift,
the creator of the greatest
prize,
valuable to keep.
Way beyond this
world,
buried deep.

SAFE SECURE PLACE

A safe, secure place called life.
Inside, it is hidden,
beneath the hatred.
Buried beneath the pride.
It is far away
from deception, deceit, and lies.
It is the absolute truth.
All the puzzle pieces.
It is joy, happiness
that never ceases.
Everything is in
a positive flow
The signals are strong.
Steadily moving in growth.
Not weak or slow.
It is the location
of the overflow.
There is a pouring
of more
than enough
but not material stuff.
It is the riches of the spirit
that resonates from
your consciousness.
If you listen,
you can hear the best,

timeless messages
that strengthen the soul.
Limitless, more
valuable than gold.
Healing and anointing
to walk bold.
A tonic and potion
making you never grow old.
An all-access pass,
an invite, you
do not want to miss on,
an environment that says,
this is it.
A nourishing retreat,
where all is
in divine order
that transcends time and space.
A SAFE SECURE PLACE!

DYNASTY

I am the descendant
from a dynasty.
Circumstances and situations
cannot destroy my legacy.
I believed in my spirit,
knowing I am free.
Guided by the marvelous
light of truth and unity.
Not allowing the oppressor
to detain the true me.
Owning my power,
over my mind, spirit, and body.
Seeing the chains
as only minor distraction
to bind me.
I hear the powerful
voices of my ancestors,
hiding from view, saying
they cannot find me.
You are not lost.
we are walking with thee.
You are safe and protected
Keep walking with dignity.
Do not allow them
to transfer hate

within your energy.
Do not let them
tell you who to be.
Do not allow them
to enter your dynasty.

DIVINE ENCOUNTER

Balanced by the divine,
I was thinking
about the way
my
life had turned.
Unable to stratify
my mind,
always feeling
overwhelmed and burned.
Having a negative force within
this old soul,
weighing me down,
clouding my judgment,
distorting my view,
everything my ancestors
had created or found.
Oh, to be a
damsel in distress,
walking in the natural realm,
which is truly a mess?
Forgetting the great, "I AM"
acting as if you
do not know him.
Feeling down
yet his presence lingers.
Angels are dispatched

to watch over you.
A disconnected powerhouse
that is inside you,
ready to renew.
No current, yet
in a state of shock.
Thinking, not knowing
what to do.
Living, yet feeling
like you have died.
Then you are introduced
to someone that makes
you feel brand new alive.
DIVINE ENCOUNTER!

THE GIFT OF LIFE

The gift of life,
it's so very precious.
It can be lived
without becoming.
Overwhelmed with strife,
paying a price.
It is to be valued.
So, we must reflect,
and use our wise mind.
Slow it down,
and think twice.
So we do not have to stress
value that perfect gift.
Keep it strong!
Don't see it as less.
Know that the gift
was given to us
to bless.
Sometimes it is
not very long.
If that is your belief,
experiences can be deep.
Nevertheless, the gift of life
is precious to keep.

FOUND MY SELF

I was making decisions
that led me down a path,
that led me down a tunnel,
that led me to a cave,
where it was dark.
Uncertain and unpredictable,
I did not realize it,
until I came to myself,
and realized
that I had taken
the wrong path.
I had the wrong mindset.
Had gotten to the place
of the wrong thinking.
My heart was sinking,
not knowing what to do.
Hoping for a miracle,
a huge break, though
the darkness made
me afraid.
I didn't know how
I could be saved.
I knew I was divinely made.
I knew great spirit
could get me
out of this place.

So, I paused, stopped,
surrendered, and meditated,
on what it means
to be safe.
Strengthened my faith.
and found me
in a better place.

THE INNER CHILD

Imagine that the inner child
is behind a door.
Where the cares of life
has caused that child
to be afraid to
open the door.
The child is filled
with anger,
feels under pressure.
So early in life,
has paid a
tremendous price,
has determined they cannot
take it anymore.
Filled with panic,
thoughts of suppression
weighed down.
Lost, looking to be found.
Keeps acting out,
unable to learn from
the lessons in life.
Ask what is this about.
How can I be
a winner of the prize?
Feel better inside,
release a healed,

renewed,
restored,
inner child.

REGULATE

It is time for me to regulate.
Change my course.
I have been doing the most.
But I do not see results.
I am always left with the question.
What is up
with my life?
How can I grow, maximize
feel more better inside
and not feel like
I want to hide,
behind the mask?
To feel like
a winner,
not feeling left out
not missing out on
the grand prize.
I feel an array of emotions,
like being in the grand ocean
of life, searching
for a ship to rescue me,
to help me navigate,
get back on course in life,
before it is too late.
I need to regulate.

MAGNIFICENT

I have opened the door
of magnificence.
I have toiled,
sometimes asking,
where it has gone
in my life.
I see others.
Believing, so balanced inside,
yet I keep searching,
trying to find,
looking into the four
corners of my mind,
the original blueprint,
not understanding where
my truth has gone.
It is buried down.
I keep looking.
But I am lost.
Not found.
Who is the keeper?
It keeps getting buried deeper.
So much time is spent.
Lower the veil
to see and restore
my magnificence.

WOMAN OF THE CROSS

There are some things going on,
I feel it, I sense it, I know
deep inside of me,
it's hard for me to understand.
There is so much more
for me to know.
I am looking for that door,
where there's healing
and so much richness,
so much more.
I have to gather my thoughts,
find my way,
keep walking.
Understand what's true.
What is right?
Understand that I'm divine.
I have that feminine power.
I can make it.
I can evolve.
I can adapt.
My energy radiates strength.
I know I have value.
I have to reaffirm
that good things do happen
even when you feel lost.
I can access my beliefs,

knowing I am
a woman of the cross.

WANDERING

There's a lot of movement
in my life.
It uses my energy.
It consumes my thoughts
and my feelings too.
Sometimes, I just don't
know what to do.
My mind goes back and forth,
like the ocean water
splashing on the shore.
I can't lower the
anchor on the ship.
It is rocking back and forth.
I'm afraid it just might tip
over, causing me to slip
back into the wrong thinking,
causing a sinking
in my innermost being,
not seeing the right course,
which way to go,
keeping me isolated
from so much more.
How can I gain my balance
and calm things down?
Stop all the triggers,
dwelling in my mind.

I need to turn off the alarm
so that I can activate my calm
and not ponder.
I want more of a positive journey,
not just to wander,
but also wonder.

SONGBIRD

I am a little songbird.
I know about the creative
power of words.
Each word is so valuable.
As it goes out with
the breath of life.
Do you know?
Words can
shape your life.
Words can affect
your energy,
interfere with your mind,
make you feel
that you're not free.
You can't see your way.
You're unable to
have a good day.
Pay close attention
to what you say
to yourself.
It just might cause you
to pay,
especially if your words
go the negative way.
So, reverse your day,
and radiate beauty

through your words
like the songbird.

USHERING THE SPIRIT

I am calling
the Great Spirit
to stay with me
so I can see
the true me,
while on this journey
that we are moving
to our destiny.
At our core
the center is,
the intention
to be free,
yet I keep
thinking.
What is this about?
What is it not?
Sometimes I think
I have it all
in my hand.
At times I
cannot stand,
often I think,
will the Great Spirit
Heal the Land?

FEEL

I feel energy within me,
swirling around
to ignite my being,
to get me out of
the lost and found,
to help me
walk in harmony,
to help me see
what it means
to be free.
I am awake,
conscious,
noticing things
in the present moment.
My power is strong.
My dedication is
mature and grown.
I am walking steadily.
Sometimes down a hill
with many curves and slopes,
yet I am able to feel.

SABOTAGE

I am becoming aware
as I sit here and stare
thinking of repetitious patterns
pouring out the same result,
always leading to 'so what'.
I can always start again,
and again, which has become my friend.
The only way to operate.
Time is short,
not enough time to relax,
and get things straight.
It is hard,
not so smart.
My inner self
knows what the real name is!
Sabotage.

GOOD THINGS

There is so much going on.
It is clouding my view.
I do not know who
to trust, it is just too much.
I have shifted away
to a place that is gray.
My eyes blink negativity.
I am not the same.
It is not me.
What is happening?
What could this be?
My heart is fluttering.
I am speechless.
I cannot sing.
I am separated from the
Good Things

IDENTITY

Who am I?
Does my soul
go above the sky.
Can it be released?
So that I can
walk in peace
and supply all
my emotional needs.
Open my spiritual eyes
so that I can see
infinite possibilities
of what it means
to be me
like the different
facets of a diamond.
The innermost
part of me,
shining in the light on
the path to my destiny
so I can notice.
all the parts of me:
a collage of my identity.

RAINDROPS

I see the raindrops.
There are so many.
They are my hopes.
They are my dreams.
They remind me of my youth.
They are proof
that tears are meant to be shed.
As I see the raindrops fall,
I remember to stand tall.
Be cleansed by the midst
to see each drop as a gift,
knowing that more will come.
You may ask where from
a hidden invisible place
an open created space
the unknown, the abyss
get this.
Let me tell you,
It is a secret place!
A soothing and relaxing spot
as you focus on the raindrops.

SPIRITUAL HEALING

My spirit longs for so much more.
It craves and wants to know
how did I get into the place?
Where is that special comfort space
that is all knowing
where I am peaceful,
growing like the tall redwood tree,
high above the rest,
anchored in longevity,
radiating oxygen that is so pure,
I can breathe freely,
where my mind
can stop wondering
what is the true image of me?
Is it based on my thinking?
Does it quench my thirst?
Does it align with my being?
Is it All Knowing,
All Seeing?
Is it a special feeling,
Spiritual healing?

NUMBNESS

I AM NUMB!
Things and experiences
are happening so fast.
I do not think
I am going to last.
I am consumed
by the past.
The present is filled
with empty gifts.
I am waiting, looking
for more positive shifts
in my life.
Like kindness,
Like respect,
Like my first, yes.
Still searching,
nothing yet.
I feel restricted.
I cannot move.
I have not been able
to get into the right
groove or flow.
I am responding,
stopped at a green light,
but I cannot go,
move ahead.

I do not know.
I am not dumb.
It is because
I am numb.

The Place

There is a place
filled with serenity,
ease and effortless peace.
Open the rooms
to your soul.
Turn up the light
to illuminate the
dark and to
warm the cold.
Change the environment.
Do not allow anyone
to stay for free,
to kill your destiny.
Get everything in order.
Remove all the bother.
Look into your eyes.
Look at your face.
Does it match
the dark space?
Can you find
within yourself
the place?

QUEEN

I was living my life,
peaceful and content.
Benefiting from my inheritance,
ever since I was born,
I was wearing my crown,
adorned from birth,
fashioned and shaped
from the earth,
under my feet.
I was a special treat,
filled with the power,
a vision
to birth a nation.
Shaped by favor, grace, and peace,
bowed down in prayer
and humility.
Speaking words,
embracing my dreams,
putting out the illusion
of less than
my true calling,
my true self
flowing like a stream,
walking between two worlds,
carrying diamonds and pearls,
valuable things,
reminiscing like a Queen

SO MUCH MORE

I deserve so much more.
When you look at me,
I am the overflow.
I have gone around the rocks
around many barriers.
I am the carrier
of my family
and ancestors' dreams
that have been
put in me.
I still stand tall.
I am strong.
I chart my own destiny,
and I can say
sometimes life is
like a movie,
with so many roles,
a distinctive character
each day,
or like a plant
with so much
room to grow.
The wisdom in all of this
is I am
so much more.

RESTORATION OF LOVE

Just imagine if
there was a restoration
all based on love.
If we could improve
our lives and reconnect
from above or within,
so that we could start
this thing all over,
and begin to show
the agape, the unconditional.
How we were
before the sin.
Let's release the potion
to each and everybody
of love,
so that we can begin to heal,
so that we can begin to grow,
so that we can pick up
our bed and walk
away from the shore,
and get into the healing stream,
and have an evolution,
where everyone can
fulfill their dreams.
In life, there is always hope.
In life, we can function above

and not below.
In life, there may be challenges,
but we can still grow.
My belief in this
is pretty sure.
Love is a powerful potion
that can spread
like wildfire,
touching the heart
of many.
We have to be
in it to win it.
It is the gift of
the restoration of love

LIFT

I am feeling
better now.
I get it,
my thoughts are
more positive,
my emotions
are more calm,
my mind is focused
on the good,
away from the harm,
away from alarms
in my life.
I get excited each day,
finally things are
going my way
I feel like
I've been passed
up in life
I feel that I kept
climbing upstairs,
only to get more strife
I'm feeling better now.
I have unwrapped a gift
that is so powerful.
It is like an elevator,
a lift.

Glory

Have you ever
Seen, felt, or learned
about the glory of life?
Has life always been tough,
where you felt penalized,
always playing a price?
What has been your story?
What has been
the central themes?
What has been the
dream snatchers
taking you out of the flow
out of the stream?
What are ways you can ignite
to get out of this struggle,
to get out of the fight?
How can you illuminate
the darkness
by ramping up the light?
What if life continues to flicker
with no stable ground?
What if it goes up and down?
What is the solution?
What answers can be found?
How can I upgrade
my life story

to a place of glory?